CANADIAN URDU LANGUAGE TEXTBOOK SERIES

Urdu
for Children: Book Two

(Grades II and III)

Let's Write Urdu
Part One

Chief Editor and Project Director
Dr Sajida S. Alvi

Coordinators
Farhat Ahmad, Faruq Hassan, and Ashfaq Hussain

Writers
Humaira Ansari, Firdaus Beg, Rashida Mirza, Hamda Saifi, Zahida Murtaza

Illustrator
Rupert Bottenberg

T0272231

McGill-Queen's University Press
Montreal & Kingston • London • Ithaca

© Holder of the Chair in Urdu Language and Culture, Institute of
Islamic Studies, McGill University, 2004
ISBN 0-7735-2761-3

Legal deposit third quarter 2004
Bibliothèque nationale du Québec

Printed in Canada on acid-free paper

This book has been published with the help of funding from the
Department of Canadian Heritage, Multiculturalism Programs.

McGill-Queen's University Press acknowledges the support of
the Canada Council for the Arts for our publishing program. We
also acknowledge the financial support of the Government of
Canada through the Book Publishing Industry Development
Program (BPIDP) for our publishing activities.

National Library of Canada Cataloguing in Publication

Urdu for children: book two / chief editor & project director,
Sajida S. Alvi.
(Canadian Urdu language textbook series)
For grades 2–3.
ISBN 0-7735-2765-6 (Stories and Poems part one)
ISBN 0-7735-2766-4 (Stories and Poems part two)
ISBN 0-7735-2763-x (Let's read Urdu part one)
ISBN 0-7735-2764-8 (Let's read Urdu part two)
ISBN 0-7735-2761-3 (Let's write Urdu part one)
ISBN 0-7735-2762-1 (Let's write Urdu part two)
1. Urdu language – Textbooks for second language learners –
English speakers. I. Alvi, Sajida S. (Sajida Sultana), 1941–
II. Series.
PK1973.U745 2004   491.4'3982421   C2004-902666-6

CONTENTS

English Section

The Story Behind This Project
Acknowledgments
Writing Practice

Urdu Section

THE STORY BEHIND THIS PROJECT

The remarkable story of the Urdu Instructional Materials Development Project began in 1986 when I returned to McGill University as the first appointee to the Chair in Urdu Language and Culture after an absence of nine years from the Canadian scene. During the time I had taught at the University of Minnesota (1977–86), the concept of multiculturalism was developing roots and taking concrete shape through Canadian government policies. The government's Heritage Languages Program, under the auspices of the Department of Multiculturalism, began sponsoring the development of instructional materials in a variety of heritage languages. On my return to Canada, Izhar Mirza, then president of the National Federation of Pakistani Canadians, and the late Muinudin Muin, both community leaders and friends, drew my attention to the need to develop proper Urdu language instructional tools for children. Consequently in May 1990, with funding from the Department of Multiculturalism, we held a one-day conference at McGill University, jointly sponsored by the Federation of Pakistani Canadians and the Institute of Islamic Studies. Its purpose was to assess the need to develop instructional materials in Urdu and to look for people to work on this project. A team of writers and coordinators was established. Thus began the arduous work of a group of individuals, divergent in their backgrounds and professional training but united by a deep sense of mission. Undeterred by difficulties of commuting from Montreal and Ottawa, and within Metropolitan Toronto, the Project team worked for long hours on the weekends and holidays for over seven years to produce two sets of books. In the initial stages of the project, I realized that the members of the writing team who joined the enterprise had the invaluable experience of classroom teaching in the public school system but no experience of writing and publishing. This did not discourage us, however. Through their sheer determination, motivation, and willingness to write several drafts of each story until everyone was satisfied, the team of full-time teachers in the Ontario Boards of Education was transformed into a team of proficient creative storywriters and authors. This was a very gratifying experience for me.

In August 1997, the Urdu Instructional Materials Development Project team members and various Boards of Education in Ontario involved in the project celebrated the Silver Jubilee of the multicultural policy of the Government of Canada with the publication of *Urdu for Children: Book One*. This groundbreaking work, which provides instruction in Urdu for children, is comprised of two volumes of texts accompanied by two audiocas-

settes, a workbook, and a teacher's manual. This work was the first of its kind in terms of the quality of its content, its sensitivity to the needs of children between the ages of four to six in the Canadian environment, and its eclectic combination of traditional and whole-language instructional methods.

This publication was seen as a fitting testament to the commitment of the Department of Multiculturalism to producing quality instructional materials for Canadian children through the International Languages Programme. This programme demonstrates that, while the English and French languages represent the linguistic duality of this nation, there is a place for other international languages, including Urdu, in the rich Canadian mosaic. For the Project team, it was also a way of joining in the celebration of the Golden Jubilee of the birth of Pakistan, where Urdu is the official language of a nation of over 140 million people.

The current book in the series, *Urdu for Children: Stories and Poems*, while similar to the first in methodology, is designed to meet the needs of children between the ages of seven to eight and older. The students' level is based on their facility in reading, writing, and speaking the language rather than their chronological age. The scope of the topics is wider than in Book One, and the forty stories and poems (most of them original and some adapted) are more complex and longer, and the original artwork is richer and more varied. More details are given in the section "About This Book." The English-Urdu and Urdu-English vocabulary lists are more comprehensive than for Book One. Two volumes of *Let's Read Urdu* have been added to help children enhance their reading skills. The two-part *Let's Write Urdu* workbook provides practice exercises in writing and reinforces the new vocabulary introduced in the texts. The *Teacher's Manual* is a comprehensive, activities-based guide for teachers and parents and provides detailed lesson plans for each Urdu text. Two carefully recorded CDs accompanying the two volumes of the textbook, ensure standard pronunciation of words and intonations in sentences, and infuse life into the stories. Original music was composed for the poems, with melodies created for children to sing to help memorize the poems. From the inception of this project, we have kept in mind the needs of children as well as the needs of those parents who have some familiarity with the Urdu language and who wish to be involved in helping their children learn the Urdu language.

The *Urdu for Children* Textbook Series was envisioned as a model that could be adapted for other non-European heritage languages, especially for South Asian languages such as Hindi, Bengali, Punjabi and languages of predominantly Muslim regions such as Arabic, Dari, Persian, Pashto and Sindhi. The Project team sincerely hopes that this vision will be realized in the coming years by the next generation of teachers and policy-makers. It would be a small but significant step in furthering the spirit of multiculturalism by promoting pride in the many Canadian cultural identities. The development of proper instructional materials for the Urdu language shows the commitment of Canadians of Indo-Pakistani origin to safeguarding their rich cultural heritage for future generations. There has been a rapid

growth in the South Asian community in Canada, a majority of whom have come from the Indo-Pakistan subcontinent where Urdu/Hindi is used as a lingua franca. In the 1986 census, the number of Canadians of South Asian origin was 266,800;* by 1991, it was 420,295, an increase of 57.5 per cent. In the 1996 census, the number jumped to 670,585, an increase of 59.5 per cent; and in the 2001 census the number has jumped to 963,190, an increase of 43.6 per cent. We hope that *Urdu for Children: Book One* and *Book Two* will help meet the needs of a rapidly increasing younger generation of the Urdu/Hindi-speaking community in Canada, the United States, and Europe.

The Urdu Language Textbook Series is the first step towards helping children develop Urdu linguistic skills so that they can keep the flame of their heritage and culture alive. In today's global village, knowledge of a third language, and particularly a non-European language such as Urdu, can certainly help Canadian children become proud and self-assured adults and a unique asset to Canadian society. Indeed, cultural and linguistic diversity can be a major source of enrichment in any social and political order. Thomas Homer-Dixon's warning that, in the current race for globalisation, languages and cultures are disappearing at an alarming rate is noteworthy. Such languages, he argues, should be protected and preserved because we need cultural and linguistic diversity to help solve our problems and resolve our conflicts, in the same way that we need varied ecosystems.**

Sajida S. Alvi

* Pamela M. White & Atul Nanda, "South Asians in Canada," *Canadian Social Trends* (Autumn, 1989): 7–9.

** Thomas Homer-Dixon, "We Need a Forest of Tongues." The *Globe and Mail*, July 7, 2001.

ACKNOWLEDGMENTS

Many institutions and individuals have worked on this project since its inception in 1990. Judy Young, the erstwhile director of the Heritage Languages Programme in the Department of Multiculturalism, ardently supported the project. The Canadian government's generous grant through her department resulted in the inception and completion of *Urdu for Children: Book One* and *Book Two*. Two other major partners in this venture are the former North York Board of Education (now part of the Toronto District School Board) and the Institute of Islamic Studies at McGill University. The North York Board and those involved in the International Languages Programme supported the project's housing, administration, and funding in addition to hosting regular meetings of the Project team members at the administration building. Among many individuals who worked at the North York Board of Education, special thanks go to Barbara Toye, Armando Cristinziano, and Susan Deschamps for their help and advice in the preparation of applications for funding to Ottawa, submission of progress reports, and careful preparation and implementation of the terms of various contracts signed by the Project team members.

The Institute of Islamic Studies has given substantive and material support to this project since my appointment to the endowed Chair in Urdu Language and Culture in 1986. This included secretarial help, bulk photocopying, postage, long-distance telephone calls, etc., as well as enthusiastic support for the book launch upon the completion of *Book One* in the fall of 1998. My frequent travel to Toronto for meetings with the Project team became part of my routine at the Institute. The publication of *Book Two* would not have been possible without the Institute's generous financial support. This timely assistance is gratefully acknowledged.

For the smooth field testing of the materials, our thanks are due to the following Boards of Education: in Metropolitan Toronto, York Region, North York, and Peel Boards, and in Ottawa, the Carleton Board. Special thanks go to these members of the Steering Committee: Irene Blayney (Carleton Board), Dr. Marcel Danesi (University of Toronto), Armando Cristinziano and Barbara Toye (North York Board), Izhar Mirza (National Federation of Pakistani Canadians), and Joseph Pizzolante (Etobicoke Board).

On substantive matters, Marcel Danesi, professor of Italian studies, University of Toronto, and James Cummins, professor of education at the Ontario Institute for Studies in Education, made invaluable contributions. The team is especially appreciative of Professor

Danesi's enthusiastic support of the project and his specific suggestions on methodology. He helped the team prepare the first lesson plan (for *Book One*) that was used as a model and has taken a keen interest in the project through the years.

Above all, I must acknowledge the unwavering commitment of the writing team members: Humaira Ansari, the late Firdaus Beg, Rashida Mirza, Zahida Murtaza, and Hamda Saifi. Their multiple roles did not deter them from putting in endless hours writing original stories and preparing creative lesson plans. The second phase was initiated in the beginning of 1993 while the work on the first phase was in its final stages. During the five-year period from 1993 to 1998, the entire group (the writing team, the project director, and the coordinators) spent long days together on weekends and holidays, evaluating and selecting the stories and revising, reviewing, and editing six or seven drafts of each story before field testing. Similarly, the lesson plans were also judiciously reviewed several times before their acceptance.

A special note in memory of Firdaus Beg, an imaginative, compassionate, and conscientious member of the team who fought cancer very courageously during the second phase of the project. In between her frequent visits to the hospital, she made sure to attend the meetings and put her heart and soul into the stories she wrote and the lesson plans she prepared while she was on sick leave from her school. Firdaus lost her valiant fight against cancer on March 17, 2002. The Project team dedicates this set of books to her. She is sorely missed.

Rupert Bottenberg, an artist in Montreal, showed the same commitment to the project as his counterparts in Toronto and Ottawa. Faruq Hassan's translations of the Urdu texts into English helped Rupert overcome the linguistic and cultural barriers, and he impressed the team with his creative and insightful interpretations of the stories through his art. Our special thanks to Rupert for the beautiful and detailed illustrations of the stories, poems, and flashcard vocabulary.

Farhat Ahmad, Faruq Hassan, and Ashfaq Hussain, the coordinators, were the anchors of our writing team. They ably supported the team in every aspect of the project. It was truly well-coordinated teamwork. In addition to my overall responsibility for the Project, Farhat Ahmad and I were intensely engaged in critiquing and editing the original Urdu stories by the team members and the lesson plans for the Teacher's Manual; Ashfaq Hussain and Faruq Hassan reviewed the stories, and typed them for field testing; Faruq Hassan compiled and typed the vocabulary lists; and Ashfaq Hussain spent endless hours in preparing camera-ready copy for McGill-Queen's University Press. Heart-felt thanks to them.

Our deep appreciation is due to those who worked equally hard to impart and preserve an important dimension of children's culture and heritage through sound and music. Jawaid Ahmad Danish and Uzma Danish brought the text of thirty stories to life through their audio recording in narrative style, providing auditory experience to complement the written text. And Nadeem Ali, an accomplished composer and singer, created background music for the

stories and composed original music for the ten poems; he spent endless hours training a children's chorus for the musical versions of some poems, sang some poems solo, and also accompanied the children with sweet rhythms and melodies.

Anwer Saeed Ansari's help is gratefully acknowledged for providing handwritten Urdu sentences and vocabulary for writing-practice exercises for field-testing, and for his help in the preparation of camera-ready copy of *Let's Write Urdu* and *Let's Read Urdu*.

The long list of individuals who shaped and helped produce this work would not be complete without thanking the following: Saqib Mehmood, Institute of Islamic Culture, Lahore, for his assistance in getting the entire manuscript of the Urdu text computer-printed on short notice; Gavin McInnes for scanning the whole project (approximately 600 pages); Nargis Churchill for preparing disks of the camera-ready copy of all volumes except the *Teacher's Manual*; Robert Cameron for doing additional layout; Suroosh Alvi for giving advice on technical matters concerning printing and music recording, and for facilitating access to the artistic and technical talent available in Montreal; and Khadija Mirza for patiently typing several revisions of the *Teacher's Manual* and Introductory sections.

Special thanks as well to the McGill-Queen's University Press and its staff for their keen desire to publish this unusual work. Philip Cercone, executive director, appreciated the significance and intrinsic value of this project all along. This was particularly evident when the Press did not receive the expected publication subsidy from the Department of Multiculturalism in Ottawa and Philip was obliged to raise funds for this publication from various sources. Susanne McAdam, production and design manager, ably steered the course of production, and Joan McGilvray, coordinating editor, edited the English sections of the project and provided helpful suggestions on format and content.

The editor gratefully acknowledges permission to reprint the following copyrighted material: Orca Book Publisher, P.O. Box 5626, Postal Station B, Victoria, BC v8r 6s4, Canada, for "Maxine's Tree," and Shān al-Ḥaqq Ḥaqqī, for his published poem, "Bhā'ī Bhulakkar.

Sajida S. Alvi

WRITING PRACTICE

OBJECTIVES

To help the children enhance their writing skills.

To show the children the mechanics of writing in Urdu script.

To make the children aware of words and spaces.

STRATEGIES FOR THE INSTRUCTION OF WRITING IN URDU SCRIPT IN THE CLASSROOM

- in the beginning of the fall term, review the letters of the Urdu alphabet and have students practise joining letters to form words.

In subsequent sessions

- Have the children sit at the desks with pencils and exercise books.

- Choose five familiar words with the same initial letters or the same final letters from the current lesson.

- Demonstrate how each word is written, one word at a time, on the chalkboard or on the chart.

- Draw arrows to show the direction of each stroke.

- After writing each word, ask the students to copy it in their exercise books.

- When all five words have been copied, ask the children to write them three or four times.

The above practice will help the children to do the homework assigned using the *Let's Write Urdu* workbook.

STRATEGIES FOR WRITING PRACTICE IN URDU AT HOME

- Encourage children to practise writing in *Let's Write Urdu*, one page at a time.

- If the children have difficulty writing, make a larger copy of the words from *Let's Write Urdu* and ask them to trace over them and then copy them.

- Give the students a few words at a time until they are comfortable with writing Urdu script.

- Regular practice (at least 15 minutes, three times a week) will help develop fluency in writing Urdu script.

Rashida Mirza

Note: In some Urdu words, the variation in spelling (as, for example, in the word and پیسا) has also been introduced.

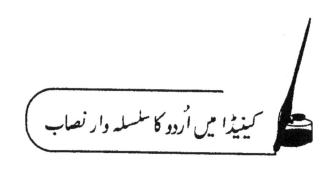

کینیڈا میں اُردو کا سلسلہ وار نصاب

بچّوں کے لیے اُردو کی دوسری کتاب

آئیں اُردو لِکھیں

(پہلا حصّہ)

معاونین

مدیرِ اعلٰی

فرحت احمد۔ فاروق حسن۔ اشفاق حسین

ڈاکٹر ساجدہ علوی

مجلسِ مصنّفین

حمیرہ انصاری۔ فردوس بیگ۔ رشیدہ مرزا۔ حامدہ سیفی۔ زاہدہ مرتضٰی

تزئین کار : روپرٹ بوٹنبرگ

فہرست مضامین

آؤ میلے چلیں

حامدہ کے اِسکول میں میلہ ہونے والا تھا

حامدہ کے اِسکول میں میلہ ہونے والا تھا

حامدہ کے اِسکول میں میلہ ہونے والا تھا

حامدہ کے اِسکول میں میلہ ہونے والا تھا

اِسکول میں میلے کی تیّاریاں زوروں پر تھیں

اِسکُول میں میلے گی تیّاریاں زوروں پر تھیں

اِسکول میں میلے کی تیّاریاں زوروں پر تھیں

اِسکول میں میلے کی تیّاریاں زوروں پر تھیں

نشانہ بازی

مچھلی

بچّہ

اِشتہار

بالٹی

دوست کے گھر

راشد نے پانی کی ٹونٹی کھولی

راشد نے پانی کی ٹونٹی کھولی

راشد نے پانی کی ٹونٹی کھولی

راشد نے پانی کی ٹونٹی کھولی

پانی کی ایک بُوند بھی نہ نِکلی

پانی کی ایک بُوند بھی نہ نِکلی

پانی کی ایک بُوند بھی نہ نِکلی

پانی کی ایک بُوند بھی نہ نِکلی

_____

_____

_____

_____

_____

نلکا

کُنؤاں

ٹنکی

ٹونٹی

چارا

بارن

ڈربہ

انڈے

تم بھی بچّے ہم بھی بچّے

کھیل رہے ہیں بہت سے بچّے

کھیل رہے ہیں بہت سے بچّے

کھیل رہے ہیں بہت سے بچّے

کھیل رہے ہیں بہت سے بچّے

سب رنگوں کے سب نسلوں کے

کے نسلوں سب کے رنگوں سب

کے نسلوں سب کے رنگوں سب

کے نسلوں سب کے رنگوں سب

_____

_____

_____

_____

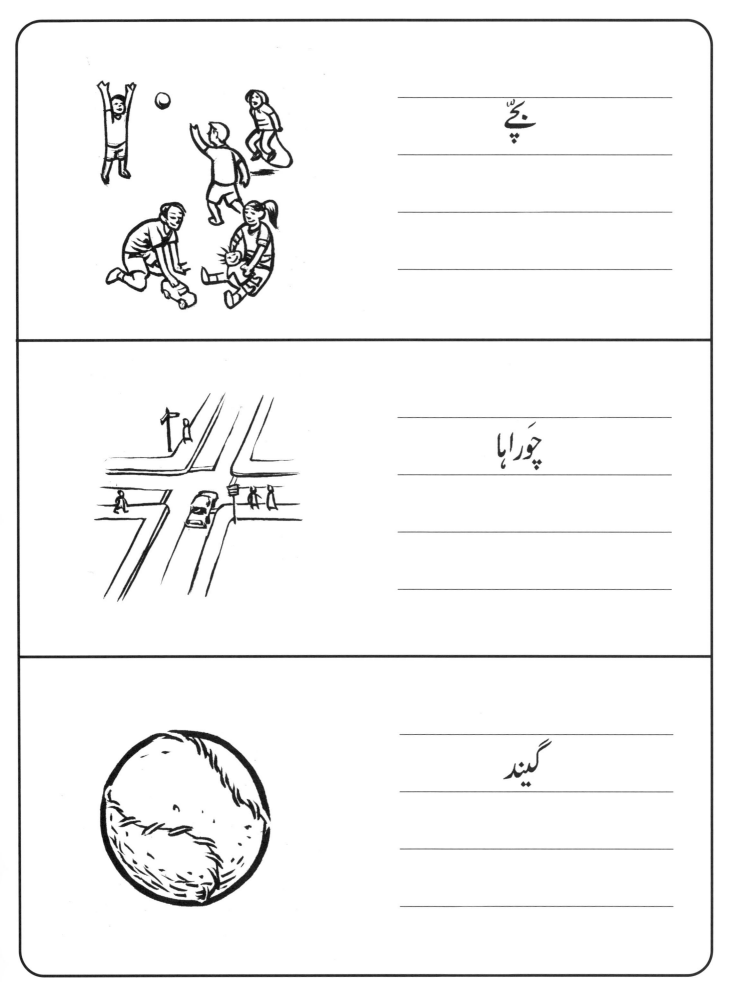

بچّے

چَوراہا

گیند

بلّا

گُلشن

پُھول

17

آسیہ کا اسکول

آسیہ نیلے رنگ کا لباس پہنے ہوئے تھی

آسیہ نیلے رنگ کا لباس پہنے ہوئے تھی

آسیہ نیلے رنگ کا لباس پہنے ہوئے تھی

آسیہ نیلے رنگ کا لباس پہنے ہوئے تھی

اُس کے گھنگھریالے بال چمک رہے تھے

اُس کے گھنگھریالے بال چمک رہے تھے

اُس کے گھنگھریالے بال چمک رہے تھے

اُس کے گھنگھریالے بال چمک رہے تھے

_____

_____

_____

_____

کینیڈا کا جھنڈا

صومالیا کا جھنڈا

اِسکول

ماسٹر صاحب

اُستانی

اِسکیٹنگ

جمیل کی کلاس خلائی مرکز جانے والی تھی

جمیل کی کلاس خلائی مرکز جانے والی تھی

جمیل کی کلاس خلائی مرکز جانے والی تھی

جمیل کی کلاس خلائی مرکز جانے والی تھی

خلائی   جہاز   کھڑکی   کے   سامنے   رُک   گیا

خلائی   جہاز   کھڑکی   کے   سامنے   رُک   گیا

خلائی   جہاز   کھڑکی   کے   سامنے   رُک   گیا

خلائی   جہاز   کھڑکی   کے   سامنے   رُک   گیا

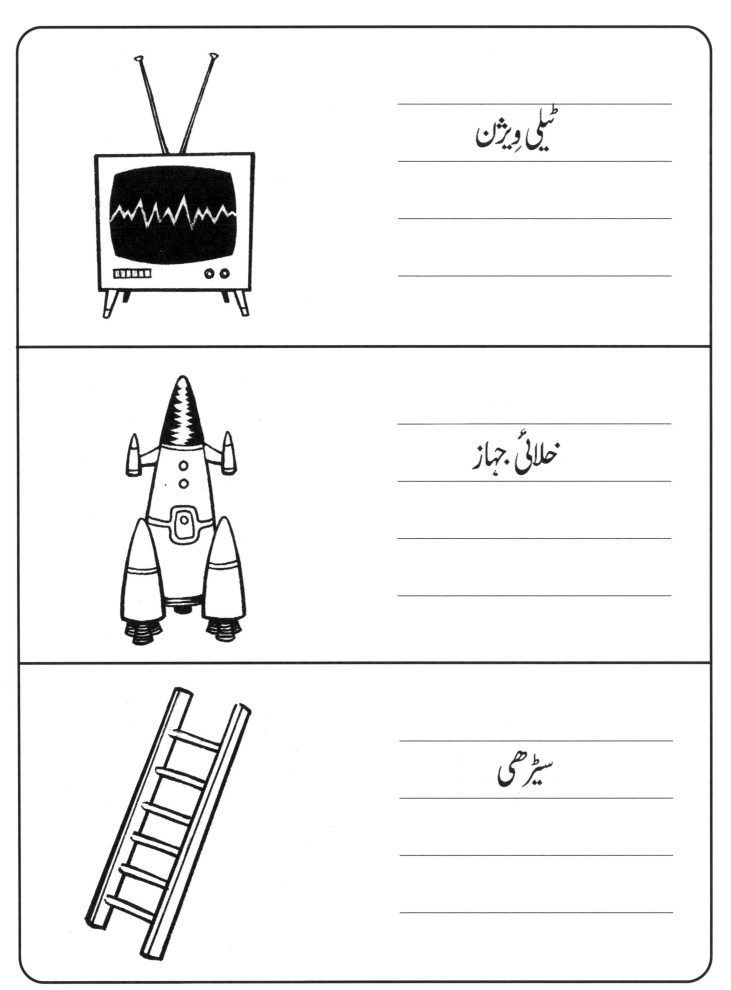

ٹیلی وِیژن

خلائی جہاز

سیڑھی

میرا دوست کمپیوٹر

ناہید   کا   کمپیوٹر   معمولی   کمپیوٹر   نہیں   تھا

ناہید   کا   کمپیوٹر   معمولی   کمپیوٹر   نہیں   تھا

ناہید   کا   کمپیوٹر   معمولی   کمپیوٹر   نہیں   تھا

ناہید   کا   کمپیوٹر   معمولی   کمپیوٹر   نہیں   تھا

_____

_____

_____

_____

_____

کمپیوٹر کی اِسکرین پر بہت سارے کھیل آگئے

کمپیوٹر کی اِسکرین پر بہت سارے کھیل آگئے

کمپیوٹر کی اِسکرین پر بہت سارے کھیل آگئے

کمپیوٹر کی اِسکرین پر بہت سارے کھیل آگئے

کمپیوٹر

کمرہ

کمپیوٹر کا کھیل

برف کا طوفان

ڈبّو گلہری کی آنکھ آج جلدی کھل گئی

ڈبّو گلہری کی آنکھ آج جلدی کھل گئی

ڈبّو گلہری کی آنکھ آج جلدی کھل گئی

ڈبّو گلہری کی آنکھ آج جلدی کھل گئی

وہ بڑے اِطمینان سے اپنے گودام میں گئی

وہ بڑے اِطمینان سے اپنے گودام میں گئی

وہ بڑے اِطمینان سے اپنے گودام میں گئی

وہ بڑے اِطمینان سے اپنے گودام میں گئی

_____

_____

_____

_____

طُوفان

ڈبّہ

مَوکھا

صبح کی آمد

اُٹھو سونے والو کہ میں آ رہی ہوں

اُٹھو سونے والو کہ میں آ رہی ہوں

اُٹھو سونے والو کہ میں آ رہی ہوں

اُٹھو سونے والو کہ میں آ رہی ہوں

ہوں رہی پھیلا میں زمانے اُجالا

ہوں رہی پھیلا میں زمانے اُجالا

ہوں رہی پھیلا میں زمانے اُجالا

ہوں رہی پھیلا میں زمانے اُجالا

_____

_____

_____

_____

اَذان

مُرغ

چڑیاں

پَر

صُبح

دُم

گلا

مشرِق

سیب اور پیٹھے

بچّے اُچھل کُود کر خُوش ہو رہے تھے

بچّے اُچھل کُود کر خُوش ہو رہے تھے

بچّے اُچھل کُود کر خُوش ہو رہے تھے

بچّے اُچھل کُود کر خُوش ہو رہے تھے

نانی اماّں نے سیب کی پائ بنائ

ناَنی اماّں نے سیب کی پائ بناَئ

ناَنی اماّں نے سیب کی پائ بناَئ

نانی اماّں نے سیب کی پائ بنائ

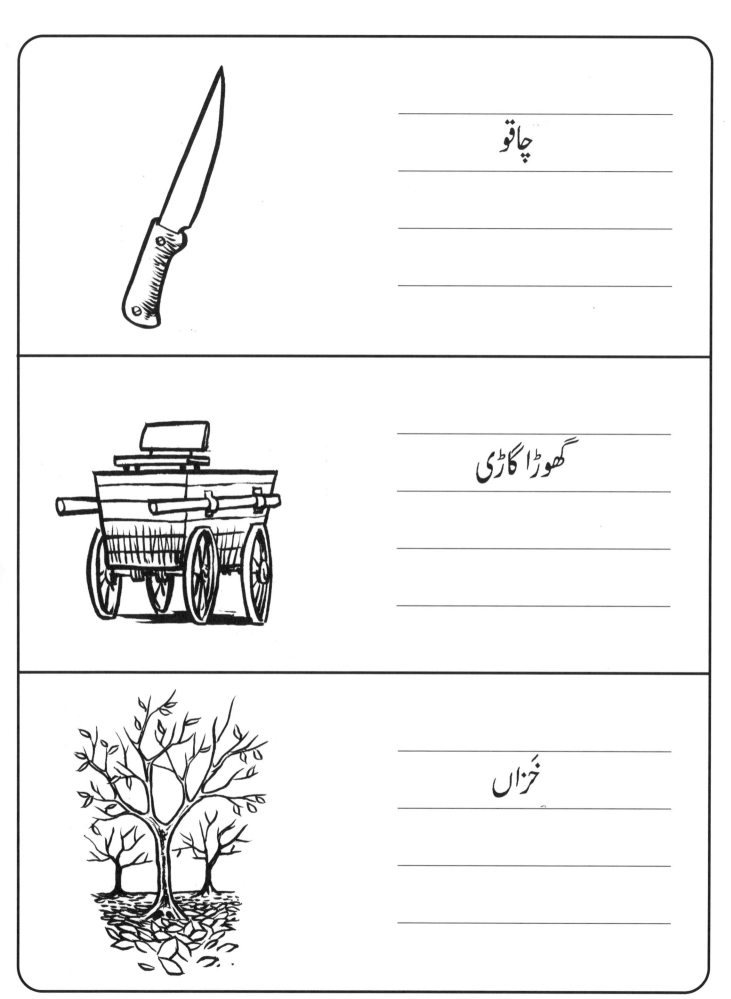

چاقو

گھوڑا گاڑی

خَزاں

سیب

پیٹھا

ٹوکری

ہوں   آتا   میں   سارو   رے   چل   چل

ہوں   آتا   میں   سارو   رے   چل   چل

ہوں   آتا   میں   سارو   رے   چل   چل

ہوں   آتا   میں   سارو   رے   چل   چل

ہوں   کرتا   باتیں   سے   چڑیوں

ہوں   کرتا   باتیں   سے   چڑیوں

ہوں   کرتا   باتیں   سے   چڑیوں

ہوں   کرتا   باتیں   سے   چڑیوں

_____

_____

_____

_____

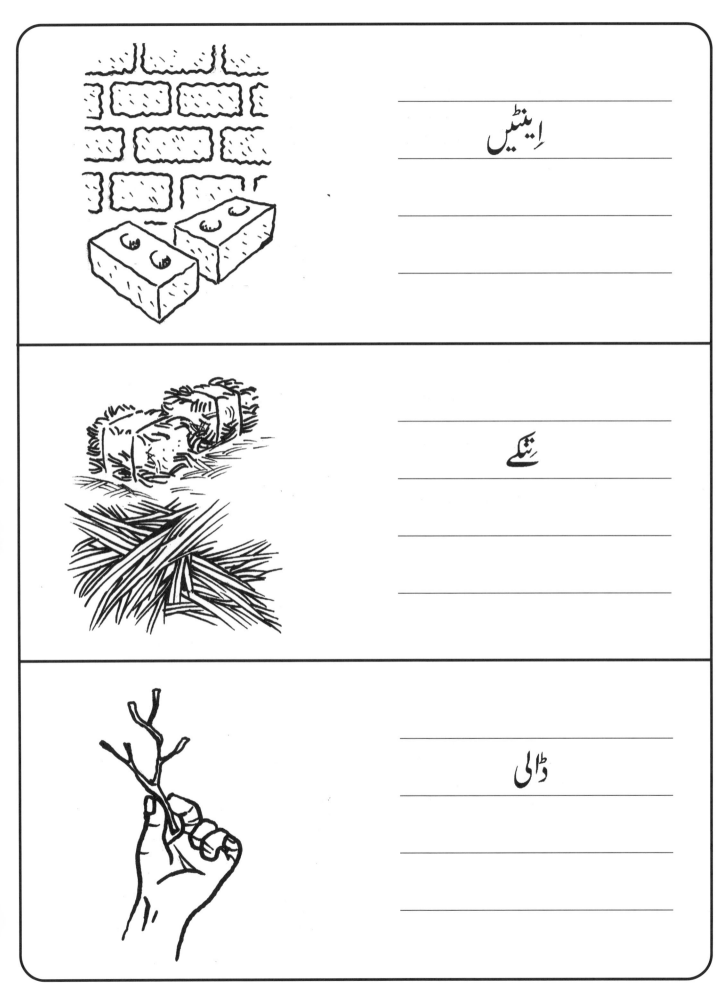

اِینٹیں

تنکے

ڈالی

سارس

مینڈک

کوّا

اُس نے خطرے کے الارم کا بٹن دبا دیا

اُس نے خطرے کے الارم کا بٹن دبا دیا

اُس نے خطرے کے الارم کا بٹن دبا دیا

اُس نے خطرے کے الارم کا بٹن دبا دیا

عُمر کو دروازے پر گھنٹی کی آواز سنائی دی

عُمر کو دروازے پر گھنٹی کی آواز سنائی دی

عُمر کو دروازے پر گھنٹی کی آواز سنائی دی

عُمر کو دروازے پر گھنٹی کی آواز سنائی دی

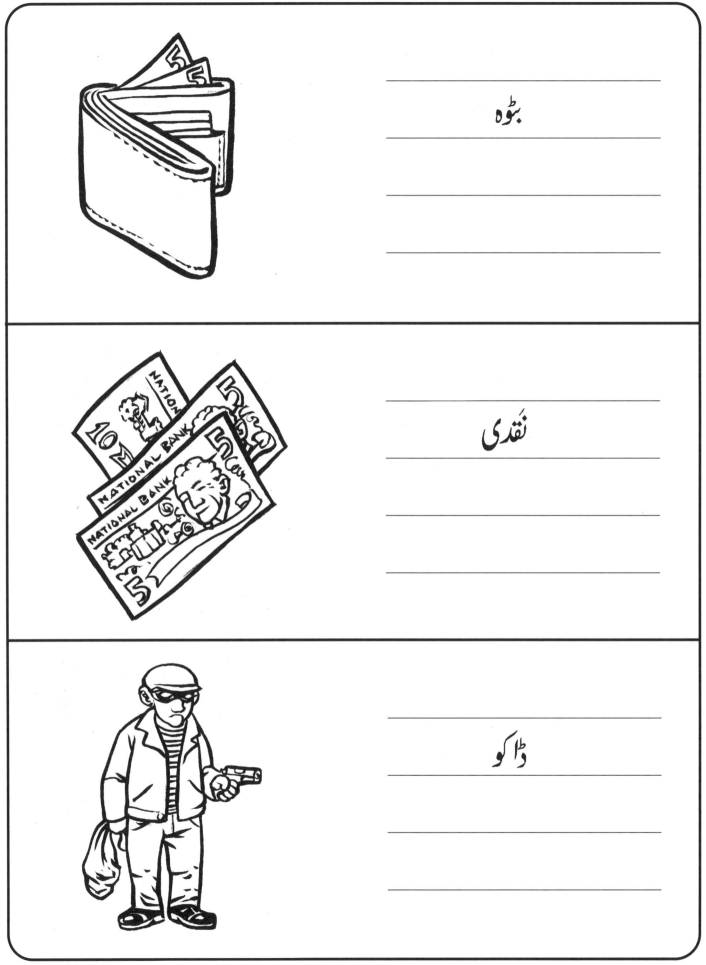

بٹوہ

نقدی

ڈاکو

لائبریری

زیور

خطرے کا بٹن

جب اُمّی غسل خانے میں بند ہوئیں

تھیں بند میں خانے غسل اُمّی

تھیں بند میں خانے غسل اُمّی

تھیں بند میں خانے غسل اُمّی

پولیس   افسر   نے   دروازہ   کھول   دیا

پولیس   افسر   نے   دروازہ   کھول   دیا

پولیس   افسر   نے   دروازہ   کھول   دیا

پولیس   افسر   نے   دروازہ   کھول   دیا

پولیس افسر

ٹیلی فون

پیچ

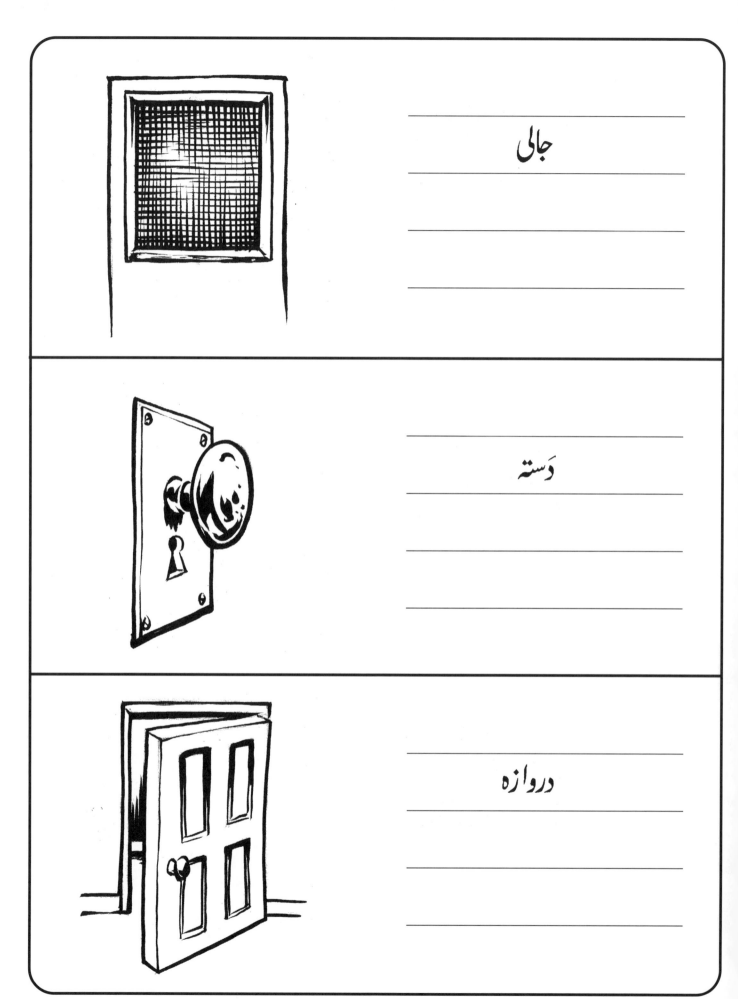

جالی

دَستہ

دروازہ

غُسل خانہ

کِھٹرکی

اپنا گھر

شہر کی رونق چل کر دیکھیں

شہر کی رونق چل کر دیکھیں

شہر کی رونق چل کر دیکھیں

شہر کی رونق چل کر دیکھیں

اپنا گھر

اپنا گھر ہے سب سے بہتر

اپنا گھر ہے سب سے بہتر

اپنا گھر ہے سب سے بہتر

اپنا گھر ہے سب سے بہتر

پِنگوئین

جوڑی

شہر

میلا / میلہ

گاڑی

ساحل

انوکھا حادثہ

دسمبر کی چھٹیاں شروع ہونے والی تھیں

دسمبر کی چھٹیاں شروع ہونے والی تھیں

دسمبر کی چھٹیاں شروع ہونے والی تھیں

دسمبر کی چھٹیاں شروع ہونے والی تھیں

_____

_____

_____

_____

_____

سب مل کر کالج کی طرف روانہ ہوئے

سب مل کر کالج گی طرف روانہ ہوئے

سب مل کر کالج کی طرف روانہ ہوئے

سب مل کر کالج کی طرف روانہ ہوئے

تالاب

کاٹیج

آئس اِسکیٹ

کمبل

برف کا آدمی

گلوبند

وہ خواب نہ تھا

ابّا نے اپنے بچپن کا ایک واقعہ سنایا

ابّا نے اپنے بچپن کا ایک واقعہ سنایا

ابّا نے اپنے بچپن کا ایک واقعہ سنایا

ابّا نے اپنے بچپن کا ایک واقعہ سنایا

بھالو کی چمکدار آنکھیں اور تھوتھنی نظر آئی

بھالو کی چمکدار آنکھیں اور تھوتھنی نظر آئی

بھالو کی چمکدار آنکھیں اور تھوتھنی نظر آئی

بھالو کی چمکدار آنکھیں اور تھوتھنی نظر آئی

بھالو

کیمپنگ

دُوربین

لالٹین

ٹارچ

تھیلا

آؤ کھیل جمائیں

آؤ آؤ کھیل جمائیں   دائیں بائیں آئیں جائیں

آؤ آؤ کھیل جمائیں   دائیں بائیں آئیں جائیں

آؤ آؤ کھیل جمائیں   دائیں بائیں آئیں جائیں

آؤ آؤ کھیل جمائیں   دائیں بائیں آئیں جائیں

گانا گائیں جی بہلائیں   جی بہلائیں خوش ہوجائیں

گانا گائیں جی بہلائیں   جی بہلائیں خوش ہوجائیں

گانا گائیں جی بہلائیں   جی بہلائیں خوش ہوجائیں

گانا گائیں جی بہلائیں   جی بہلائیں خوش ہوجائیں

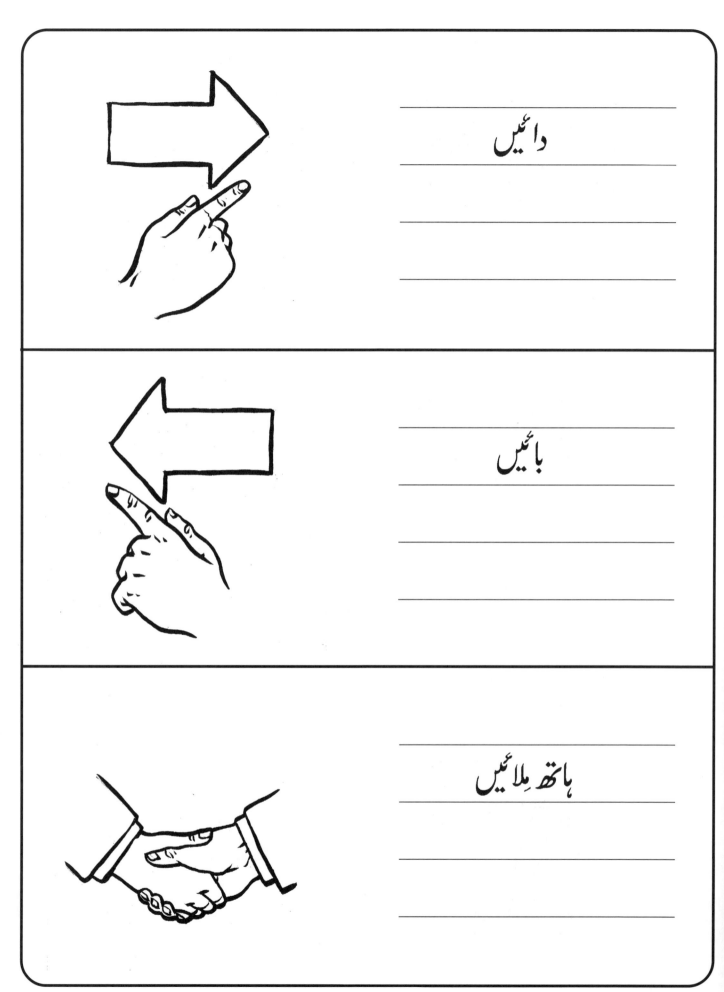

دائیں

بائیں

ہاتھ مِلائیں

گھیرا باندھیں

چکّر کھائیں

کُودیں

هوم رَن

نادر کی ٹیم بلّے بازی کر رہی تھی

نادِر کی ٹیم بلّے بازی کر رہی تھی

نادِر کی ٹیم بلّے بازی کر رہی تھی

نادر کی ٹیم بلّے بازی کر رہی تھی

_____

_____

_____

_____

_____

مخالف ٹیم کا کھلاڑی گیند پھینک رہا تھا

مخالف ٹیم کا کھلاڑی گیند پھینک رہا تھا

مخالف ٹیم کا کھلاڑی گیند پھینک رہا تھا

مخالف ٹیم کا کھلاڑی گیند پھینک رہا تھا

ایمبولینس

بَلّا

گیند

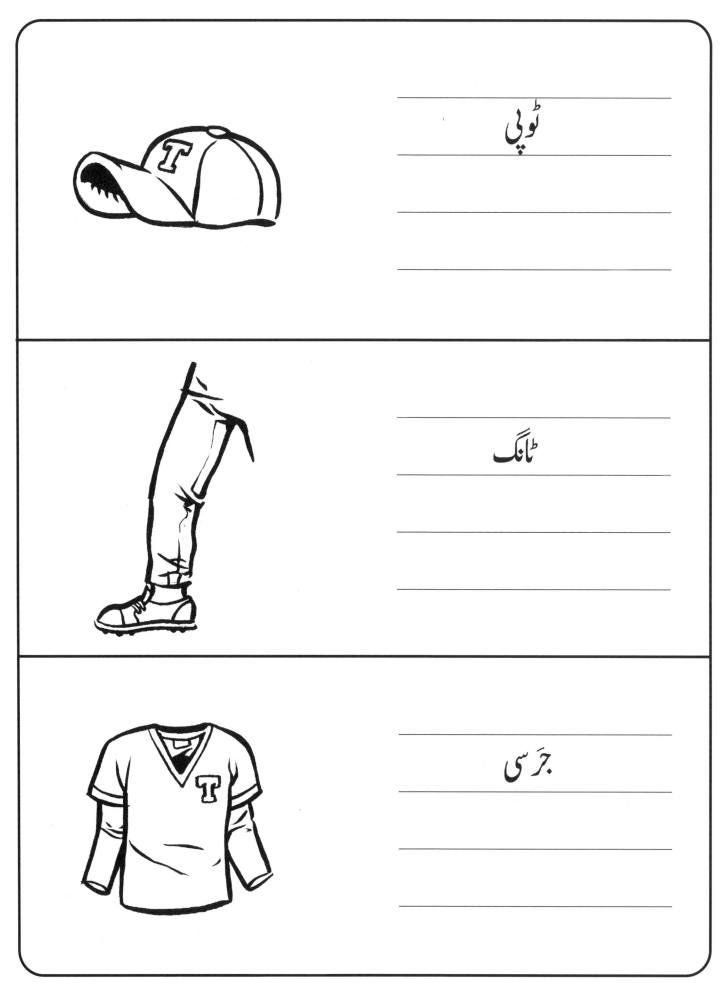

ٹوپی

ٹانگ

جَرسی

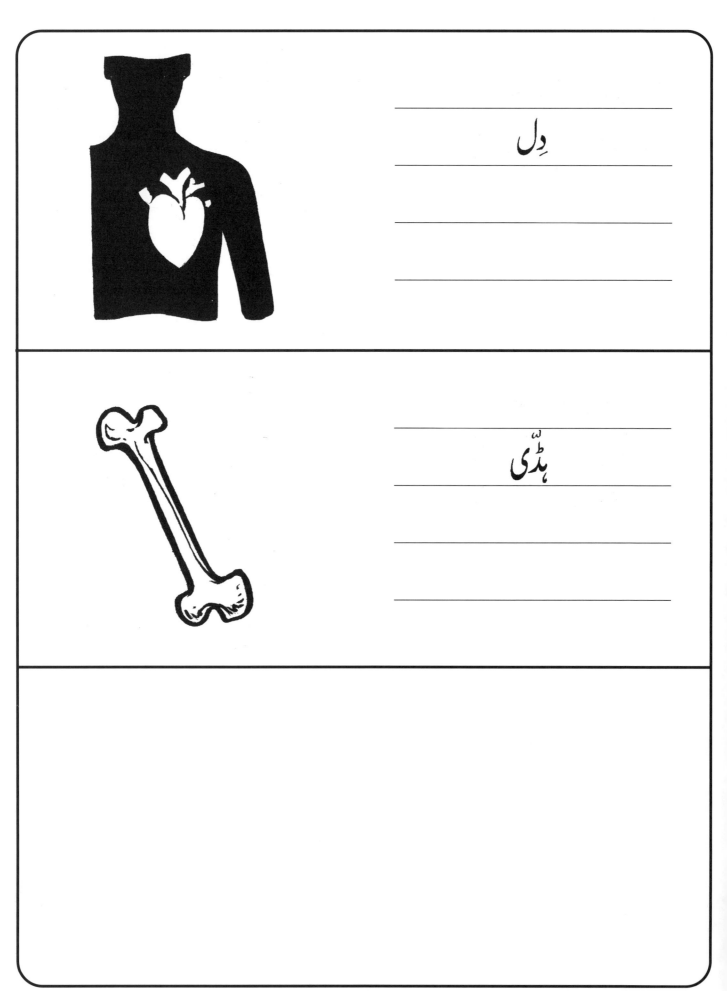

دِل

ہڈّی

بلّی اور چوہے کی دُشمنی کیسے ہوئی ؟

بلّی   کَشتی   بنانے   کے   لیے   لکڑی   لائی

بلّی   کَشتی   بنانے   کے   لیے   لکڑی   لائی

بلّی   کَشتی   بنانے   کے   لیے   لکڑی   لائی

بلّی   کَشتی   بنانے   کے   لیے   لکڑی   لائی

چوہے نے اپنے دانتوں سے لکڑی کاٹی

چوہے نے اپنے دانتوں سے لکڑی کاٹی

چوہے نے اپنے دانتوں سے لکڑی کاٹی

چوہے نے اپنے دانتوں سے لکڑی کاٹی

بِلّی

چُوہا

مَوج

جزیرہ

چَپّو

کَشتی

پھل

سُوراخ

خرگوش نے کہا میری دُم سے کانٹا نکال دو

خرگوش نے کہا میری دُم سے کانٹا نکال دو

خرگوش نے کہا میری دُم سے کانٹا نکال دو

خرگوش نے کہا میری دُم سے کانٹا نکال دو

_____

_____

_____

_____

خرگوش گائے کا چارا لے کر بھاگ گیا

خرگوش گائے کا چارا لے کر بھاگ گیا

خرگوش گائے کا چارا لے کر بھاگ گیا

خرگوش گائے کا چارا لے کر بھاگ گیا

خَرگوش

حَجَّام

گائے

دُولھا

دُلہن

تُحفہ

بُوجھو تو جانیں

ایک جانور ایسا جس کی دُم پر پیسہ

ایک جانور ایسا جس کی دُم پر پیسہ

ایک جانور ایسا جس کی دُم پر پیسہ

ایک جانور ایسا جس کی دُم پر پیسہ

سر پر ہے تاج بھی بادشاہ کے جیسا

سر پر ہے تاج بھی بادشاہ کے جیسا

سر پر ہے تاج بھی بادشاہ کے جیسا

سر پر ہے تاج بھی بادشاہ کے جیسا

_____

_____

_____

_____

_____

آسمان

مَور

ریڈیو

دِیا

بُھٹہّط